Maine Coast PERSPECTIVES

Text & Photography by Antelo Devereux, Jr.

Schiffer Publishing Ltd

4880 Lower Valley Road, Atglen, Pennsylvania 19310

Schiffer Books are available at special discounts for bulk purchases for sales promotions or premiums. Special editions, including personalized covers, corporate imprints, and excerpts can be created in large quantities for special needs. For more information contact the publisher:

Published by Schiffer Publishing Ltd.
4880 Lower Valley Road
Atglen, PA 19310
Phone: (610) 593-1777; Fax: (610) 593-2002
E-mail: Info@schifferbooks.com

For the largest selection of fine reference books on this and related subjects,
please visit our web site at www.schifferbooks.com
We are always looking for people to write books on new and related subjects.
If you have an idea for a book please contact us at the above address.

This book may be purchased from the publisher.
Include $3.95 for shipping.
Please try your bookstore first.
You may write for a free catalog.

In Europe, Schiffer books are distributed by
Bushwood Books
6 Marksbury Ave.
Kew Gardens
Surrey TW9 4JF England
Phone: 44 (0) 20 8392-8585; Fax: 44 (0) 20 8392-9876
E-mail: info@bushwoodbooks.co.uk
Website: www.bushwoodbooks.co.uk
Free postage in the U.K., Europe; air mail at cost.

Designed by Douglas Congdon-Martin
Type set in Zurich BT
ISBN: 978-0-7643-3015-5
Printed in China
Designed in the U.S.A.

Introduction

As much as anything, this book is about icons, about the places, people, and things which, for me, symbolize the midcoast of Maine. I have had the privilege of being able to vacation in Maine since my early childhood. In local parlance, I am "from away" — not born and raised in Maine — but Maine has been a significant part of my life. I like to think that "away" derives from the region's significant maritime history and remoteness, or distance, away from the centers of financial and political activity, nationally and globally. One can imagine the feelings of the captain and sailors on board, and their family members, investors, merchants, and townspeople on shore, as a ship loaded with lumber, ice, granite, or lime sailed away for distant ports, some as far away as China.

Maine's midcoast — indeed the entire coast — has a distinct and compelling character. It is defined by the people: honest, hard-working, and independent, with a wry sense of humor; by its buildings: Colonial, Federal, Italianate, Greek Revival, and Victorian, made of indigenous materials, wood, stone, and brick; by the land: hilly, grassy, forested, rocky, and splashed by the ocean; by the water: rivers, harbors, coves, ten-foot tides, and reversing falls; and by its light: clear, blue, foggy gray, with brilliant sunrises and sunsets.

The photographs concentrate on the midcoast area along Route 1 between the state's two largest navigable rivers, the Kennebec and the Penobscot. It is an area rich in colonial and maritime history. Beginning at the mouth of the Kennebec River where the Popham Colony was settled in 1607 and the first ship was constructed in Maine, they end at the Penobscot River, where a new cable-stayed bridge with its 420-foot-high observation room carries Route 1 across. With Route 1 as a connecting spine, peninsulas extend to the southeast between the Kennebec, Sheepscot, Damariscotta, Medowmak and St. George's rivers. Indeed because of its many peninsulas, islands, harbors, coves and rivers, some have called it a "drowned coast."

I hope that these images will convey a sense of Maine as I see it.

— A. D.

HISTORY

Following the retreat of the Laurentide Ice Sheet, which covered the area with several thousand feet of ice, the region has been inhabited by a succession of people. First, between 5000 and 3000 years ago, were the prehistoric Red Paint people, about whom little is known. Following them came tribes of the Wabanaki Confederation: the Abnaki's around the Kennebec River and the Penobscots around the Penobscot River.

While people from Europe and Scandinavia had been exploring and fishing in the region for some time, documented attempts at settlement did not occur until the very beginning of the 17th century. In 1607, George Popham and Raleigh Gilbert tried to establish a colony at the mouth of the Kennebec River, an area called Sagahadoc by the natives. The Popham Colony is a not widely known, because, unlike the Jamestown Colony in Virginia, it lasted barely a year. Its settlers sailed back to England on the *Virginia*, noteworthy because it was the first ship constructed in Maine.

Since then, and over the course of a couple hundred years, fishing and trading outposts were established and gradually expanded into settlements, villages, and towns. However, life, at best, was unsettled as French, English, and Native American tribes fought for control over the territory. The English claimed the land north and east of Kennebec River, while the French, from the other direction, claimed the land to the south and west of the Penobscot River. Forts and settlements at places such as Pemaquid were built, overrun, destroyed, and rebuilt several times. The Native Americans were caught in between these struggles.

Following independence came peace and stability. Maine became a state in 1820. The midcoast developed into an important maritime center for fishing and shipbuilding, because the region had three valuable resources: water in the form of rivers and bays; trees — pines, spruce and oaks; and hard-working, skilled people. For well over 100 years most of the towns on rivers and bays along the coast had shipyards. Maine-built clipper ships and large schooners regularly sailed around the world, and smaller coastal schooners exported lumber, granite, ice, and lime to the cities down the coast. Times have changed that. However, vestiges remain: the harbors, villages, farms, and houses which are the subject of the photographs in this book.

Popham Beach State Park is on the west side of the mouth of the Kennebec River and has one of the few large sand beaches on the midcoast of Maine.

Popham Beach Village. In an area once known as Sagadahoc by the Native Americans who lived here, Popham village lies on a cove between Fort Popham and Fort Baldwin. Perhaps it is fitting that the journey along the midcoast begins here where the first attempt by the English to colonize the region, the Popham Colony, occurred in 1607. It is also where the first in a long line of Maine-built ships, the pinnace *Virginia*, was launched.

Fort Popham was begun in 1861 at the entrance to the Kennebec River to protect the shipyards upstream in Bath during the Civil War, but it was never completed. It occupies the site of several earlier smaller installations constructed by both the British and Americans to protect the river.

A Coast Guard Station, Squirrel Point Light, sits across the Kennebec River from Phippsburg.

The Maine Maritime Museum is just down the river from the center of Bath on Route 209. Percy and Small, a major shipyard and builders of some of the largest sailing vessels in the 19th century was located here. A full-scale sculptural representation of the *Wyoming*, the largest six-masted schooner built by the shipyard, is under construction.

The 142-foot Grand Banks fishing schooner, *Sherman Zwiker,* is open to visitors, offering a glimpse of what it was like to have been aboard a fishing vessel. The Bath Iron Works can be seen in the distance.

The Maine Maritime Museum has both indoor and outdoor exhibits. A view looking out to the Kennebec River where the Grand Banks fishing schooner, *Sherman Zwiker*, awaits visitors.

9

Above: The iconic large cranes at the Bath Iron Works signify that the shipbuilding tradition continues.

Right: The two bridges across the Kennebec River at Bath are the 80-year-old Carlton Bridge and the seven-year old Sagadahoc Bridge. For years the Carlton Bridge lift bridge served dual purposes. It carried Route 1 above and the railroad below until 2000 when the Sagadahoc Bridge was opened to carry vehicular traffic. Trains still clatter thunderously across the older bridge.

Old cups recycled as bird baths outside of one of Bath's shops.

Downtown Bath offers an array of restaurants, galleries, shops, and bookstores, as well as a small park and marina on the Kennebec River.

Sculpture in one of the residential gardens.

Many of the houses along Bath's tree-lined residential streets, not far from the river, were constructed during the town's booming 19th century maritime economy. Some have been turned into B&B's or offices.

Above: Owned by Sagadahoc Preservation, Inc., the historic Winter Street Church, now called the Winter Street Center, is home to the Studio Theatre of Bath. It is an example of creative reuse of significant historic buildings.

Right: Like Popham Beach on the other side of the Kennebec River, Reid State Park has one of the few large sandy beaches on the midcoast of Maine. It is off Route 127 at the end of Georgetown Island, on the east side of the Kennebec River.

Five Islands is an intimate harbor at the end of Route 127 on Georgetown Island. As its name suggests, the harbor is formed by five islands that enclose it.

The picturesque town of Wiscasset is situated on the west of Wiscasset Bay, an enlargement of the Sheepscot River. At one time it was the largest deepwater port in New England. In 1813 the bay was recommended as a site for a naval yard because of its capacity to handle many large vessels of deep draught. Wiscasset was the home port for the auxiliary schooner *Bowdoin* which carried Capt. Donald B. MacMillan on his arctic explorations.

The Federal-style Nickels-Sortwell house was built in 1807 by Capt. William Nickels who was a ship-owner and merchant. It is a testament to the prosperity that was growing in this and other coastal communities involved in maritime trade. The house became a hotel in the 1830s and was later purchased by Alvin Sortwell as a summer house. It is now owned and operated by Historic New England and is a National Historic Landmark.

This sunken garden is planted in the cellar of two buildings that were successively destroyed by fire: The Whittier Tavern, built in 1766 and burned in 1843, and its successor, Hilton House. Frances Sortwell bought the property, created the garden and gave it to the Town of Wiscasset.

Left: Castle Tucker, another house surviving from the burgeoning 19th century maritime economy, sits on a hill and overlooks the Sheepscot River and Wiscasset Harbor. It was constructed in 1807 and is now a Victorian museum operated by Historic New England and open to the public during the summer. Rumor has it that people are afraid to pass by the house at night because of the many ghost stories associated with it.

Above: Lincoln County Museum and Jail was in active use as a jail between 1811 and 1954, and even served as the State Penitentiary between 1820 and 1824. The structure — walls and floors — is entirely made of impenetrable stone. Graffiti, which date back to the 19th century and depict such things as ships and a navigational map of the world, can be found on some of the cell walls.

Above and left: The Musical Wonder House, just down High Street toward the center of town from Castle Tucker, contains an entertaining and comprehensive assortment of 2000 music boxes and mechanical instruments. The house was built in 1852 as a double, or two-family, house. It now is owned by Danilo Konvalinka, who founded the museum in 1963.

Red's Eats often has a line of people waiting to enjoy a lobster or crab roll. This famously popular spot is situated on Route 1 at the bottom of the hill in Wiscasset.

The town of Boothbay lies about 30 minutes out Route 27 from Route I. This peninsula, on the east side of the Sheepscot River, is split by Boothbay Harbor into two arms — Southport Island and East Boothbay.

The Coastal Maine Botanical Gardens are situated on about 250 waterfront acres in Boothbay and offer a variety of experiences including beautiful gardens, native wildflowers, marvelous stonework and rock plantings, pristine forest, and lovely water views. Walks can be taken along the central gardens' paths or the long trails that extend beyond.

The Chiseled Orb, by Henry Richardson, is just one example of the many pieces of sculpture that add delightful accents along the Coastal Maine Botanical Gardens' paths.

Above: Capt. Sawyer's Place is one of many places to stay in and around popular Boothbay Harbor. The harbor is one of the more active ones along the coast and is a departure point for whale-watching trips and cruises to Monhegan Island. The town is also home to an excellent aquarium and the Bigelow Laboratory for Ocean Sciences, which specializes in the study of biological productivity of marine food webs.

Left: The replica of *HMS Bounty*, which was originally constructed in Lunenburg, Nova Scotia, for her star role in the 1962 movie, *Mutiny on the Bounty,* has just been completely overhauled at Boothbay Harbor Shipyard and is being prepared to head out to sea. It is not unusual to see larger vessels, whether sailing or motor yachts, being serviced in this busy harbor.

Above: The Boothbay Harbor Memorial Library is a World War I memorial and an example of the Greek Revival architecture that can be found throughout the midcoast region. Here the library is decorated in advance of Independence Day. It was originally built as a private house in the 1840s.

Right: A long, wooden footbridge, which connects one side of the harbor with the other, is an excellent place to take a walk and view the harbor. The triangular truss supports the old swing draw bridge, which is no longer operable.

Above: Out Route 27 from Boothbay Harbor a swing bridge marks the crossing onto Southport Island. Not far from the bridge is the Southport General Store.

Left: The Cuckolds lighthouse, which marks the entrance to Boothbay Harbor, can be seen from a small harbor at the tip of Cape Newagen on Southport Island. Nearby is the Newagen Seaside Inn.

Above: East Boothbay is yet another town with a shipbuilding history, and the tradition continues. Here an ocean-going tugboat is undergoing repairs at one of the town's boat-building facilities.

Right: Ocean Point is just beyond East Boothbay. Soon these chairs will be filled with people relaxing and taking in the view of boats moving in and out of Boothbay Harbor.

Right: St. Patrick's Church is located a couple of miles outside of New Castle and is the oldest Catholic church in New England, having been founded in 1808.

Below: New Castle lies directly across the river from Damariscotta. The four-spired tower of the Second Congregational Church is visible from Route 1.

Damariscotta is located at the intersection of Routes 1 and 29 and is at the navigational head of the Damariscotta River. Like many other towns along the coast, Damariscotta was a shipbuilding center in the 19th century. With the influx of wealth from this activity, Federal, Italianate, and Greek Revival houses were built, many of which remain today. The town has a range of shops, galleries, and places to eat and stay including the Maine Coast Book Shop & Café.

Above: 19th century cast ironwork over a doorway

Right: Kayaking has become an increasingly popular way to explore the coastal waters, and many places to rent or purchase kayaks can be found.

Just upriver from Damariscotta are a pair of shell middens. These dumps are primarily composed of oyster shells, deposited here by a succession of Native American people between about 2000 BC and 1000 AD. This view down river was taken from the Whaleback Shell Midden, which is a Maine State Historic Site. Prior to its use as a mine for chicken feed in the late 19th century, the midden was about 30 feet deep, 1600 feet long, and 1300 to 1600 feet wide. The oyster shells on the bottom layer ranged from 12 to 20 inches long.

Above: Water lilies, a common sight on freshwater ponds, glisten in the sun near Pemaquid.

Right: Barns come in many colors, but red is one of the more common ones. This one is between Walpole and Damariscotta on Route 129 on the way to Pemaquid Point

36

Left: Not far from Pemaquid is the town of South Bristol. Its picturesque working harbor lies on both sides of Route 129, which crosses a drawbridge. Adjacent to the bridge is Osiers Wharf, where a visitor can find a tasty sandwich or lobster. Further down Route 129 is Christmas Cove, another harbor worthy of a visit.

Below left: The Pemaquid Lighthouse, built in 1827 and reconstructed in 1857, marks the entrance to Muscongus Bay. The tower is open to the public, and the view from the top is worth the 34-foot climb. Monhegan Island can be seen about 20 miles in the distance.

The reconstructed bastion and ruins of Fort William Henry are located on the Colonial Pemaquid Historic Site just off of Route 129 near Pemaquid Neck. Home to a sizable Wabanaki Native American settlement dating back at least one thousand years, colonial Pemaquid became the site of an early 16th century English outpost and fishing station. The original fort was erected at great expense in 1692 to replace its predecessor, Fort Charles, after it and the Pemaquid settlement were felled by an Indian attack in 1689. Nearby are the excavated ruins of the Pemaquid Colony, which was established in the 1620s as a fishing and trading post.

The Hotel Pemaquid, opened in 1888, is one of several comfortable and hospitable facilities located at the ends of the coastal peninsulas, where people can get away and enjoy the ocean views.

Above and following page: Pemaquid Point

Left: Between Round Pond and Pemaquid Point sits New Harbor, a small working harbor. As is the case in many harbors, one can eat a seafood dinner on the deck at Shaw's Fishing Wharf while watching activity in the harbor.

Above: A three-pound lobster with its claws safely held shut with rubber bands.

Right: Blueberries, like lobsters, are a Maine icon. When in season during the summer, wild ones can be found for sale almost everywhere.

On Route 32 outside of Waldoboro, a magical world abounds with animals, birds, fish, and various other imagined objects made from discarded pieces of steel. Here is wonderful example of Maine artistic craftsmanship and ability to make use of leftovers.

Right: Early morning view of one of the many farms along Route 32 from Waldoboro to Pemaquid Point. The Medowmak River is in the distance.

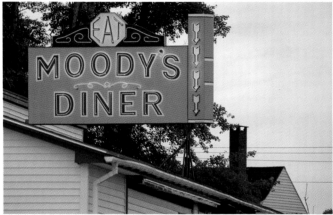

When it's time for breakfast, lunch, or dinner, numerous cars can be seen gathered outside of Moody's Restaurant in Waldoboro, testimony to the quality of the food and service they have provided since P.B. Moody opened a restaurant in 1930.

Waldoboro was another significant shipbuilding port during the 19th century. The town is situated at the navigational head of the Medowmak River and lays claim to the first-ever five-masted schooner, the *Governor Ames*, which was launched in 1888. The town is just off of Route 1 on Route 220. It was named after General Samuel Waldo who was the proprietor of the Muscongus Patent granted in 1630 for the right of exclusive trade with the Native Americans.

Left: An early morning view of the Medowmak River between Waldoboro and Friendship, where it flows into Muscongus Bay. Because the river has some tricky bends and turns, the newly built schooners were towed downstream from Waldoboro to a place not far from here, where they could set off under sail.

Above: The German Protestant/Lutheran Church just outside of Waldoboro on Route 32 was founded in 1792 and is one of the three oldest churches in Maine. Germans were said to have been recruited by General Samuel Waldo to help settle his 576,000 acre grant.

Left: Whether the need is for groceries, sandwiches, coffee, a soda, or some gas, general stores are found throughout the coastal area and inland. While they are privately owned and operated, collectively they form a friendly and reliable "chain" of convenience stores that serve their local communities and passersby. This one is in the town of Friendship.

Below and opposite: Friendship is a working harbor on Muscongus Bay at the intersection of Routes 97 and 220. The town gives its name to the Friendship Sloop, which was gradually developed around the latter part of the 19th century to meet the needs of the bay's fishermen. The sloops varied in range in size from 21 to 50 feet.

Left and above: The Olson House gained its fame from having been depicted in Andrew Wyeth's famous, if not iconic, 1948 painting, *Christina's World*. The house, located not far off River Road on Hathorne Point in Cushing, is now part of the Farnsworth Museum and is open to the public.

Apple orchards — some old, some new — abound in Maine. This one is behind the Olson House in Cushing.

From what was a trading post in 1630 emerged a town with a significant history and wealth of shipbuilding, maritime commerce, and lime production. Here is one of the few buildings reminiscent of its maritime past, while, nearby, boat building continues at the Lyman-Morse boatyard.

River Road leads from Cushing to Thomaston. Historically Cushing has been somewhat of a haven for artists. One of them was Bernard Langlais, a sculptor and painter, who created this large-scale wooden sculpture.

A house and barn on one of Thomaston's residential streets just up hill from the harbor.

Ten to twelve foot tides along the coast are a part of life here. Sometimes in well-protected harbors boats will be seen sitting on the bottom at low tide.

Thomaston sits at the navigational head of the St. Georges River, up which explorer George Waymouth traveled on June 12, 1605. It is believed he set a cross to establish England's claim to the lands around. The inscription on the base of this commemorative cross says: *"That we, the menne of Englande, have marked this spot for home. And if they dare uproot it God turn it to their loss! Beside Saynte George's River we left Sainte George's crosse"*

Montpelier, clearly visible from northbound Route 1 outside of Thomaston, is a replica of a house built by General Henry Knox after he retired from serving as Secretary of War under George Washington. The original house situated on a large estate fell into disrepair and was torn down to make room for the railroad right-of-way.

The morning Maine Eastern Railroad train crosses the St. George's River in Thomaston on its way back to Rockland from Brunswick. This is one of many water crossings made by the railroad on its picturesque route between the two cities.

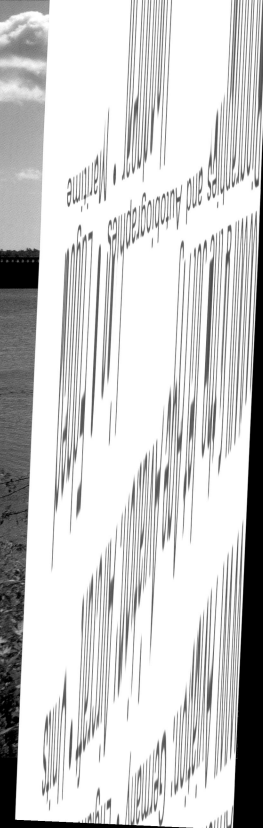

Port Clyde is one of the access points for Monhegan Island, which is a popular spot for artists and writers as well as tourists. During the summer months the Monhegan Boat Line operates three boats per day. A one-way trip to the island takes approximately an hour.

Containers of bait ready for use in lobster traps are a familiar scene in many of the small harbors which can be found along the coast. These happen to be on Spruce Head.

Port Clyde is a significant, picturesque, and historic fishing harbor situated in the town of St. George. On the waterfront, Port Clyde general store offers a good supply of groceries, wine, sandwiches, coffee, etc. for local residents, visitors, and boaters alike. There also is a seafood restaurant, gift shop, and, up the street, an ice cream store. A number of noted artists have worked or work in the area, including N.C. Wyeth and Greg Mort.

The Marshall Point Lighthouse was built in 1857 at a cost of $5000 and marks the entrance to Port Clyde and Muscongus Bay. It is one of several along the coast that feature walkways or brides from the keeper's house on the shore to the lighthouse situated a distance away. Tom Hanks ended his cross-country run in the movie, *Forrest Gump*, here.

The Owl's Head Transportation Museum is located at the Knox County Airport just outside of Rockland. It features an interesting, notable, and worthy collection of almost anything mechanical that is old — airplanes, cars, trucks, and motorcycles.

The museum is a popular destination for hobbyists, who drive and fly their classic vehicles here for frequent weekend rallies in summer. In addition, during the warm months the museum is host to various shows, meets, and auctions that feature transportation machines.

The view from Owl's Head can either be there or not. Islands appear and disappear, depending upon the whimsey of fog. Sometimes a bit of fog can enhance the view.

The Owl's Head Lighthouse was built in 1825 to mark the entrance to Rockland Harbor in response to the growing lime trade in the area. The stairs that climb to the light from the keeper's house were once covered to protect the way during adverse weather conditions. It is located off of Route 73 in Owl's Head State Park.

Rockland was a major transportation hub and shipbuilding and fishing town. Here trains met the steamboats, large ships were constructed, and tons of deep sea fish were processed. Today its harbor still serves as a connection point for ferries between mainland and the islands, as well as a jumping off place for coastal cruises. It is successfully undergoing a major rejuvenation and is host to many art galleries and wonderful places to eat.

Right: Every year the town puts on its 4-day Maine Lobster Festival during which approximately 20,000 pounds of lobsters are consumed. The town also hosts the annual Boats and Harbor Show. The Farnsworth Museum and its Wyeth Center also are located here.

Left: A gong from a navigational aid, once was sounded by the motion of the waves.   61

The Rockland lighthouse marks the entrance to Rockland Harbor. Sitting at the end of a mile-long breakwater, it watches over the windjammers, small cruise ships, fishing boats, and ferries headed out from the harbor to the islands beyond.

At one time Rockland was a major ship-building and shipping center. The clipper ship *Red Jacket* was built here, and until recently she held the record of slightly over 13 days for the fastest Atlantic crossing from New York to Liverpool for a sailing vessel.

Right: Schooners, whether on a harbor cruise or headed out to the islands, pass by the breakwater. It offers close-up views of them under sail (wind permitting).

There are few places where one can walk seemingly on top of the water for close to a mile. The breakwater, which protects Rockland's Harbor, is one such place. A stroll out to the lighthouse is an invigorating way to "be out on the water" among the boats without leaving dry land. Constructed during the last decade of the 19th century its huge stone blocks came from Vinalhaven, an island in Penobscot Bay famous for its granite.

Between Rockland and Camden, just off Route 1, lies Rockport. It derives its name from having been the site of extensive lime quarries and kilns a century and a half ago. The town and its harbor were also engaged in shipbuilding, some of which continues today. Rockport Marine built a replica of *Godspeed*, which was launched in 2006 to help commemorate the 400th anniversary of the Jamestown colony in Virginia. The town is also home to the Maine Photographic Workshops, just up the hill from the harbor, as well as to some windjammers.

Andre, the famous harbor seal and subject of a movie, "summered" in Rockport. He has since passed on, but his memory remains in the form of Jane Wasey's sculpture, which overlooks the harbor.

Harbor seals, once close to extinction in this region, can be seen now and then sunning themselves or swimming about looking for their next snack.

These restored lime kilns in Rockport are the last surviving physical evidence of Rockport Harbor's industrial past. The production of lime for mortar and plaster was a major industry in the area. It continues to this day in neighboring Rockland.

An old quarry not far from Rockport and Camden.

Far left: A view of the many shops along one side of Camden's main shopping street.

Left: Camden is characterized by its busy harbor, quality shops and fine restaurants, tree-lined streets with white clapboard houses, and white church steeples. Pictured here is one of Camden's icons: the steeple of the Chestnut Street Baptist Church.

A view of the Camden Public Library from the harbor with Mount Battie in the background. Not visible, but to the Library's right, is the Bok Amphitheater, designed by Fletcher Steele, one of the country's foremost landscape architects. Beyond the amphitheater is Harbor Park, designed by the Olmstead Brothers, a firm headed by a son and step-son of Frederick Law Olmstead.

As seen from the top of Harbor Park, Camden's harbor is home to many "windjammers," or coastal schooners, which depart regularly on daytime and overnight cruises to harbors in the Penobscot Bay area. The harbor generally is crammed full of boats of all sorts. Wayfarer Marine Co., in the distance, is a major boatyard in the region, and large yachts are often seen tied up to its docks or on its ways. The people on the lawn are early birds awaiting the annual dog show.

Continuing Penobscot Bay's maritime history, coastal schooners and windjammers frequently can be seen sailing in the bay, loaded with passengers on daily or overnight trips to various harbors. While some of the windjammer fleet is comprised of original ships that hauled tons of freight during their time, most are replicas.

The Maine coast is characterized by a vast assortment of rocks that document the lengthy and fascinating geologic processes that occurred over millions of years. Forces of change are constantly at work on them, whether they be waves or the roots of spruce trees, which appear to cling to solid rock. The rocks are unforgiving should a boat run aground.

Above: Accessible by ferry at Lincolnville, the Grindle Point Lighthouse on Islesboro is reminiscent of the measures taken to ensure safe navigation along a coast made treacherous by rocks and hidden ledges. This lighthouse was erected in 1874 to replace the original one, which was built in 1851. The keeper's house is now home to the Sailor's Memorial Museum.

Right: The fog bell at Grindle Point Lighthouse is a now-silent reminder of the old-time sound and light navigational aids made obsolete by radar and global positioning systems.

When the ice sheet melted 10,000-15,000 years ago, it left behind large boulders, called erratics, which were carried many miles from their original location. While exposed at low tide, some are hidden when the tide is in and present a threat to passing boats. This one seems to take on the appearance of a bison looking west.

Above left: A common sight, especially in the spring, is lobster fishing gear assembled at the fisherman's house and waiting deployment in nearby waters.

Above right: As happens in towns and cities across the country, Islesboro villagers gather for a parade to celebrate Independence Day.

Right: A house sits quietly in the morning fog.

Above and above right: Coastal Maine historically has provided many wonderful subjects for artists. Galleries, which sell the work of some famous and not-so-famous local artists, can be found in and between towns

Right: While the water may be cold, sailing in it can be exhilarating whether in a schooner or small boat. Fresh winds make it sparkle in the afternoon sun.

The woods and marshes are as integral a part of the natural fabric of the region as are the rock and water. Many preserves have been created to save the natural environment. These valuable ecosystems also provide relaxing places for a walk.

The sun rises over calm waters in the Penobscot's east bay.

Local movie theaters can still be found in towns along the coast. This one is in Belfast.

The main street in Belfast descends to the waterfront. Once a busy commercial port, Belfast is "reinventing" itself and becoming home to art galleries and restaurants.

Weekly farmers' markets are commonly found in various towns along the midcoast. They feature locally grown produce.

The Penobscot Marine Museum's campus, on the National Register of Historic Places, encompasses many buildings along Church Street in downtown Searsport and exhibits a comprehensive display of the maritime and mercantile history of Penobscot Bay. Depicted here are the Nickels-Colcord-Duncan House, First Congregational Church, and Merithew House. Searsport, just to the north of Belfast, was home to eleven yards and to more shipmasters than any other town in America. Between 1810 and 1890, more than 200 ships slid down the ways in Searsport and in 1887 alone more than 1,200 vessels arrived in local ports.

Bayside is an historic Victorian community of small cottages and common facilities situated around a green that slopes down to the edge of Penobscot Bay. Originally constructed as a Methodist meeting camp in the late 1800s and early 1900s, many of the houses served as dormitories for the congregants.

A few miles outside Searsport is Fort Point on Cape Jellison. This was the site of Fort Pownall (1759-1775) which protected the western approach to the Penobscot River. A lighthouse now marks the way.

A 15-inch Rodman canon at Fort Knox aims across the Penobscot River near Bucksport. The fort was constructed between 1844 and 1864 to protect and defend the entrance to the river to upstream towns such as Bangor.

The recently opened, cable-stayed Penobscot Narrows Bridge carries Route 1 across the Penobscot River at Bucksport. Its observatory, 420 feet atop one of the supporting pylons, is reputed to be the highest bridge observatory in the world.

Dev Devereux has been making photographs since he was ten years old and has been a regular visitor to Maine for most of his life. He frequently can be found, with a camera in hand, searching for his next photo, whether it be along the shore, in a field, or on a city street. His work has been exhibited in Maine, Vermont, Pennsylvania, and Delaware.